# Contents

Who was Wassily Kandinsky?            4

Early years                          6

Teaching and learning                8

Experiments with colour              10

A fresh start                        12

New ideas                            14

Painting shapes                      16

Back to Moscow                       18

Teaching art                         20

At the Bauhaus                       22

The end of the Bauhaus               24

Living in Paris                      26

Final days                           28

Timeline                             30

Glossary                             31

More books to read and paintings to see    31

Index                                32

# Who was Wassily Kandinsky?

Wassily Kandinsky was a Russian painter. He is well known for his **abstract** pictures. He was also a teacher who **inspired** many other artists with his ideas.

Wassily was one of the first artists to paint abstract shapes in bright colours. His paintings don't always look like something from real life. His pictures show new ways of arranging coloured shapes.

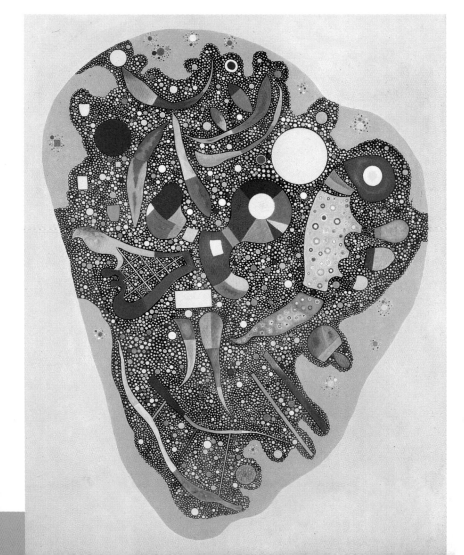

*Colourful Ensemble*, 1938

# Early years

Wassily Kandinsky was born on 4 December 1866, in **Moscow** in Russia. In 1871 his parents **divorced**. Wassily moved to Odessa, also in Russia, to live with his aunt.

In 1889 Wassily visited northern Russia. There he saw art made by the local people. He loved what he saw and began to paint pictures of the places he knew.

*The Port of Odessa*, 1890

# Teaching and learning

In 1892, Wassily married his cousin, Anya Shemiakina. A year later he began to teach at the University of **Moscow**. By 1896 Wassily knew he wanted to be an artist.

In 1900 Wassily began to study art in Munich, in Germany. There he helped start a group of artists called the 'Phalanx'. Wassily made this poster telling people about their first **exhibition**.

Poster for the first Phalanx exhibition, 1901

# Experiments with colour

In 1905 Wassily saw a special **exhibition**. All the painters there used strong colours. Henri Matisse was the leader of this group. After this, Wassily became **bolder** in his use of colour.

*The Blue Rider*, 1903

The rider in this painting is St George, **patron saint** of England. He is riding out to make the world a better place to live in. Wassily wanted his paintings to change the world, too.

# A fresh start

Wassily travelled a lot in France and Russia. In 1908 he moved back to Munich, in Germany. There his paintings became more colourful and less **realistic**.

Wassily painted this picture in Murnau, a small town in Germany. He has not tried to show us exactly what he could see. The painting is an **impression** of the view.

*Road at Murnau*, 1909

# New ideas

In 1911 Wassily helped to organize another **exhibition**. All the artists were trying to find exciting ways to paint. Wassily was even **experimenting** with writing poetry.

*Composition IV*, 1911

Between 1910 and 1939 Wassily painted ten large pictures he called 'Compositions'. This was one of the first **abstract** pictures ever painted. It is made up of shapes and blocks of colour, rather than real objects.

# Painting shapes

In 1911 Wassily and Anya were **divorced**. By 1913 Wassily had decided to paint only **abstract** shapes. His paintings were shown in New York, pictured here. People had to look carefully to see what Wassily had painted.

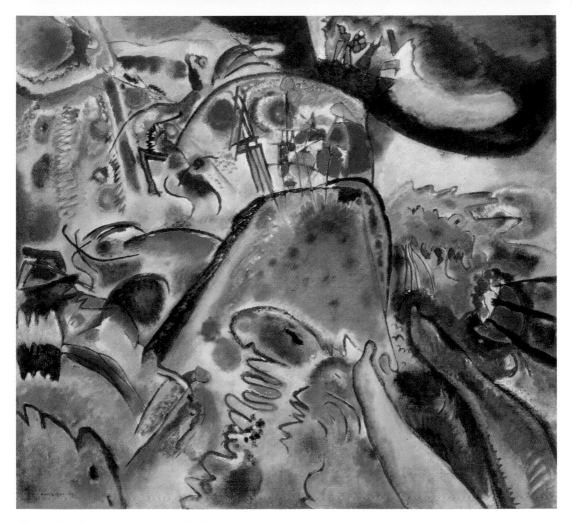

*Small Pleasures*, 1913

Wassily now tried to fill his pictures with shapes and colours. He said that this painting made him think of the sound of small, falling, drops of water.

# Back to Moscow

After **World War I** began in 1914, Wassily returned to **Moscow**. There he met Nina Andreevskaya. They were married in 1917.

When the war ended, Wassily hoped that his homeland would be a good place to live. His paintings were bright and hopeful of the future.

*In Grey*, 1919

# Teaching art

In December 1921 Wassily and Nina left **Moscow** again, to travel to Germany. Wassily began teaching at the **Bauhaus**, a famous art school. He was very excited by this.

This was one of Wassily's last Russian paintings. He was still painting coloured shapes. He often painted circles. He thought these were the most perfect shapes of all.

*Red Spot II*, 1921

# At the Bauhaus

Wassily was very busy with his teaching at the **Bauhaus**, but he also painted a lot. Other artists at the school designed furniture. One of them named this chair after Wassily.

This is one of Wassily's most important pictures from this time. The colours, shapes and spaces between them all balance together perfectly. The other artists Wassily worked with at the Bauhaus **inspired** some of his very best work.

*Composition VIII*, 1923

# The end of the Bauhaus

In 1933 **Adolf Hitler** took power in Germany. He did not like the kind of art the **Bauhaus** was teaching. The Bauhaus closed and most of the teachers moved to other countries.

This was one of the last paintings that Wassily did in Germany. He knew he would not be safe there any longer. In December 1933 he left for Paris.

*Decisive Pink*, 1932

# Living in Paris

In Paris, Wassily tried to make money by selling his paintings. These were difficult years for him. An **exhibition** held in 1937 helped more people to see his work.

In 1939 war broke out once more. In 1940 German soldiers entered Paris, but Wassily stayed in the city. He tried to carry on as normal. He still painted many well known shapes, like the red circle here.

*Around the Circle*, 1940

# Final days

Wassily became ill during the war. He still wanted to find new ways to show his thoughts in his art. He used bright colours and shapes to show what he was feeling.

*Twilight*, 1943

Wassily died on 13 December 1944. This is one of the last paintings he did. He is remembered for his work on new ways of painting.

# Timeline

| | |
|---|---|
| 1866 | Wassily Kandinsky is born in **Moscow**, Russia, on 4 December. |
| 1871 | Wassily's parents **divorce**. Wassily is brought up by an aunt. |
| 1879 | The artist Paul Klee is born. |
| 1886 | Wassily studies at Moscow University. |
| 1892 | He marries his cousin, Anya Shemiakina. |
| 1893 | Wassily teaches at Moscow University. |
| 1896 | He begins to study art seriously and moves to Munich, in Germany. |
| 1900 | Wassily studies at the Munich Academy of Art. |
| 1901 | Wassily helps to start the 'Phalanx' group of artists. |
| 1911 | Wassily and his wife are divorced. He helps organize the first '**Blue Rider**' **exhibition**. |
| 1914 | **World War I** begins. Wassily escapes to Switzerland and eventually returns to Moscow. |
| 1917 | Wassily marries Nina Andreevskaya. They have a son, Vsevdod. |
| 1920 | Vsevdod dies. |
| 1921 | Wassily and Nina return to Germany. |
| 1922 | Wassily starts work at the **Bauhaus** art school. |
| 1923 | Wassily has one-man show in New York. |
| 1933 | The Bauhaus is closed. Wassily moves to Paris, France. |
| 1939 | World War II begins. |
| 1944 | Wassily dies in France, aged 78, on 13 December. |

# Glossary

**abstract**   art which does not try to show people or things. It uses shape and colour to make the picture.

**Adolf Hitler**   German leader from 1933 to 1945

**Bauhaus**   famous art school in Germany

**Blue Rider**   group of artists in Germany, started in 1911, led by Wassily and Franz Marc

**bolder**   braver

**divorce**   to end a marriage

**exhibition**   art on display for people to see

**experiment**   to try things out

**impression**   a sense of what is there

**inspired**   when someone give good ideas to someone else

**Moscow**   capital city of Russia

**patron saint**   holy person that watches over a country

**realistic**   trying to show something as it really is

**World War I**   war in Europe that lasted from 1914 to 1918

## More books to read

*How Artists Use Shape*,
Paul Flux,
Heinemann Library

*The Life and Work of Paul Klee*,
Sean Connolly,
Heinemann Library

## More paintings to see

*Cossacks*, Wassily Kandinsky,
Tate Gallery, London

*Composition IX*,
Wassily Kandinsky,
Museum of Modern Art, Paris

# Index

abstract pictures    4, 5, 15, 16

Andreevskaya, Nina (second wife)    18, 20

Bauhaus    20, 22, 23, 24

birth    6

death    29

divorce    6, 16

Hitler, Adolf    24

illness    28

Moscow    6, 8, 18, 20

Munich    9, 12, 13

Odessa    6

Paris    25, 26, 27

poetry    14

Shemiakina, Anya (first wife)    8, 16

war    18, 19, 27, 28